THE QUEER PO

Now Say It Back

Caitlin McKenna

First published in Great Britain by Bent Key Publishing, 2022
Copyright © Caitlin McKenna, 2022
The moral right of the author has been asserted.

All rights reserved. No part of this book may be reproduced in any form or by any electronic or mechanical means, including information storage and retrieval systems, without permission in writing from the publisher, except by reviewers, who may quote brief passages in a review.

ISBN: 978-1-915320-10-0

Bent Key Publishing
Owley Wood Road, Weaverham
bentkeypublishing.co.uk

Edited by Rebecca Kenny @ Bent Key
Cover art © Samantha Sanderson-Marshall @ SMASH Design and Illustration
smashdesigns.co.uk

Printed in the UK by Mixam Ltd.

To the lovers, and the losers. Sorry, that's the way life works. You'll love again.

Contents

Preface   *vii*

Agape — Maya   11
Eros — I have a taxidermy butterfly behind glass on my wall. It's beautiful   12
Philautia — Legacy   13
Storge — Maiden Name as Comfort Blanket   14
Pragma — Let Me Make You (a latte)   16
Ludus — *I've Seen You on Instagram and I just wanted to say* Hi   17
Mania — When the Boy You Love Tells You He Wants to Die   20
Love — <3 Me (on leg)   23
Mania — Spit Kintsugi   24
Ludus — Sillage   28
Eros — Sol   29
Storge — Like White Musk and Cigarette Smoke   30
Philautia — I Know I Could Be Good   31
Philia — Ophelia Damnation   34
Pragma — Mother, Maid and Mixed Martial Arts   36
Agape — Love   37

Acknowledgements / About the Author   41
About Bent Key   47

Preface

You don't need much to understand these poems. Just to have loved — even if that's just your cat. But if you'd like a little extra information, I was inspired by the ancient Greeks and the way they theorised love. You see, each type of love — platonic, familial, committed — was seen in different ways and celebrated for what it was, something I feel we should do more often.

Because as long as I've lived, I've felt loss, pain, and loneliness — but I've always felt some type of love, and I'd really like to celebrate that, to applaud that, and to promote the acknowledgment of that in everyone. Praise the love you've received and embrace showing it to everyone in your life. Don't regret what love you've shown, even if it ended up hurting you. Love is beautiful. It's horrific. And when we are shown it, we should always say it back.

Now Say It Back

Maya

Sprawling,
with that comfortable ease.
A sense of curiosity
balanced upon such small pink pads.
Cats meow at the same frequency as newborn babies.
It's a manipulation tactic,
a way to convince us to serve and protect,
a force of their own,
tumbling from pyramids to one bedroom flats,
plastered across the walls in binary code
and lit up in pixels.
She is the closest thing I know to a God.

**I have a taxidermy butterfly behind glass on my wall.
It's beautiful.**

Lust is a butterfly. It comes to me for a flit
with wings that extend and envelop what they wish,
to suckle from nectar sweetness
and transform, with just a trickle
of what once was would remain.
Lust is a butterfly
I have seen it blossom
and flee
from what seemed secure
like leaping from rock
to supple petal,
soft to touch
with just enough resistance
to push back
and force a change,
a dash from the dish that it toyed and tongued.
Lust is a butterfly
and our friction is the wing's beat,
momentum and mad dash,
entombed in momentary wound,
womb and wisteria,
lavender unfurl
like a burgeoning bruise.

Legacy

All I want is to stand in the footprints I left myself,
when I last visited this damp place in the torrent of rain,
in the deepest puddle I've ever met I am a
squib searching for a backbone —
wonderland in which I do not negate all my
own accomplishments
or attribute them to anyone but myself. My
own voice, my own name:
I've been getting it wrong for years, never
insisting they pronounce it right
or that the 'lin' isn't silent. I would occupy all the space
and never feel guilty, allow the bareness of my skin
and refuse to apologize for the lack of decoration.
I would walk without the terror,
shave my head and refuse to let anyone braid it any more.
I have been reduced to mere muse, a phantom
of the bookshelves,
a name scribbled on passed note, occupant of whispers —
I don't dream of becoming a cautionary tale.
But when I am told I am a whirlwind of an experience,
I no longer wish to diminish the force of my
destructive might.
I am a legacy of my own making. I will leave footprints
not because they find them beautiful
but because the weight of my body,
of all my unhollow bones and fed flesh
grafted the shape upon the ground, moulded
to the unique etch of all I encompass.
Love does not equate to ownership.
But when I claim my own self
it feels a little like romance.

Maiden Name as Comfort Blanket

On the days when the frog in my throat takes over
I remind myself that the voice only I can conjure
sounds just like my grandma,
who picked strawberries and made a family,
who worked in chip shops and petrol stations
and insisted on driving the van every time we moved.
And the hands that bury nails into my white palms
resemble those of my grandad's
who placed hot water bottles in my mum's bed every night,
who would save up all his change
to buy her a colouring book at the end of the week.

Sat at chariot backseat, my mother once told me
when my grandparents started courting
he walked an extra two hours every day
to make sure she would get home safe.
I think about when I was little
how they would keep a jar of fudge in the living room
and make me cheese sandwiches to eat in the conservatory
and teach me about all the flowers in their garden.

I think about how one day
my grandma decided she wanted three birds inked on her wrist,
so, at 66 she and I walked into a tattoo parlour,
and she didn't flinch, didn't once whimper
stoic in her resolve, untouched by the pain.
Now, with midnight emblazoned on her arm,
She said *if I'm gonna get it, I'm gonna get it where they can see,*
and how she got bored of waiting to grey
and we dyed her hair in her cream-frosted bathroom,
and how she's always fifteen minutes early
but waits, tight-lipped when I'm running late.

I think about how they bicker about petty things
and he will turn his head and laugh at us when
he says *Bloody Linda*
(knowing she doesn't like it when he uses that word)
and she'll simply reply, grumpily bemoaning
Rob and I cannot help but breathe a little easier
at the familiarity of
the conversation.

And the way the love that keeps them finding
new things to argue about
runs through my veins, pumps in my heart, and
spills when I tumble.

And I swallow.

Let me make you (a latte)

She is both Aphrodite and Hephaestus
when she brings me my coffee.
Within her, I see both Love and Fire,
the way she carefully totals and grinds,
forging life force from beans and
drawing hearts in white foam.
She adds vanilla, so when I draw the mug
to my own, the warmth is sweetness, and I am
delighted. There is a softness in these moments,
in the way the bitter is cut
with the packets of sugar
sat in boxes under the stairs that we mount,
weary pilgrims to our morning wonders;
such divine joy in the clinical routine
but she makes it an art.
The marriage forges this cup
and for the first time in my life, birth is a beauty
when the outcome is this miraculous.
Affection is present when this is her first
job of the day, the first labour,
this drink is a dragon slain; simply put,
she is a God, bringer of life.
And in the rich hues of white mug stains,
I see Olympus. There is no overstating the way
I can smell heaven in this earthy aroma,
earthly potion, perfuming my clothes, my hair,
the air itself, with its sinful sustenance.

**I've seen you on Instagram and
I just wanted to say hi**

And just like that
they are radiant
and smiling down at the hummus,
I see their button nose in the chickpeas,
and the way their green eyes shine
like the sprinkles of chives
I scatter lavishly,
feeling generous.
They are apple pie, topped with cream;
they are warm *Jammie Dodger* blondies
(Novelty of the Day);
they are chilled iced chais
and the cinnamon spritz on top -
I blush,
flush pink,
blood rush,
my words stumble,
tumble as they come falling out.

Their smile knocks me off balance once again.
I trip at their feet
and enjoy my travels,
wondering haphazardly if the rainbow socks signal
like a neon sign
or whether my furious flutters are
like a siren in the morning,
waking the neighbours.
Behind shiny glass domes,
crowned like a triumph
over rose petal garland,
I lust, hungry for a taste,
out of Tantalus' reach.

I sit in silent suffering,
not knowing how to get their sparkling eyes
out of sight/
out of mind/
irises reflected in pots and pans,
and their freckles in the froth of my latte.
I hold onto the mug like a life raft
sinking into submission,
soft affection,
and simple crush.

When the boy you love tells you he wants to die

I realise within the instant that I do not want to lose him. Simultaneously, I am ecstatic at the thought of all my withering away, of starving myself until there is nothing left of me and as I too cease to exist, I will finally be bliss, having achieved what I've spent a lifetime destroying myself to create. But when I think of him feeling the same way, I am distraught.

To build him up is what I was born to do. I am not the girl he will end up with, but I will make him into the man that finds her. There is no other way to say it but that when I am cooking for him, I am fulfilled, fuelling his body for the next girl who comes along, however painful that may be. Albeit worthy — if he can be happy.

Feeling this way was not something I sought. The feeling lies in the frustration of trying to thread a needle as the fibres keep slipping past that silver eye. The boy has a smile that could break glass and I keep chewing fragments of shattered mirrors for him. Reaching for his hand always feels like it could go two ways and closing my fist on the burning tip of a lit spliff is never an option I'm eager to risk. I bandage my wounds daily with a fury, a fire, a crimson kiss, and a scarlet torn throat. I'm afraid there will always be a part of me that still holds a torch for you, as undeserving as that may be.

For the girl with new scales and an old emptiness cannot hope to be deserving of the boy with a smile that could sink a thousand ships, who could carve crystal with his collarbone to drape around her neck. She must be so pure, someone that he can adore, and devote himself to... Maybe when I have found myself again, she can become me, or rather I will transform into the one who will listen and love without lecturing or crying as he waits and bemoans the living.

I am a dead woman. I cannot bring him into the light when I am shrouded by the dark.

How exactly do you imagine yourself saving this boy and fitting into his life when he is no longer sick?

You are poison and toxic touch. Born with a hole in your heart and chasing the absence ever since. No safety when you are around. Contain yourself before you contaminate. Self-isolation sounds pretty good until you realise who it is you are locked up with.

Allow him to flourish and purge the pain. You recognised you loved him when he first told you he didn't want to be here anymore.

He cannot die when he has touched the interior of every vein, pounding through your system like the drugs you tried to use. I am cavity extracted, too torturous to have around,
splinter pervading skin, tic leeching onto calf, ingrown nail hobbling the foot, cancer of the marrow draining all, atrial spetal defect. He is transplant, tell him and trust him.

If you are looking to stay, then realise you must stay. Sort your shit. Become the living example of all he must emulate to stay alive.

When the boy you love tells you he wants to die,

stay alive. For him.

<3 Me (on Leg)

I think what I mourn the most
is that you never got to see me at my best.
When the easy wave breezes over
and I laugh at the day and tell Homeric epics
over glasses of chilled wine and brush away the unease
of the setting sun, never fearing that it won't rise again,
but revelling in the tangerine hues.
I am trial without tribulation on days I kiss the morn.

And the bed does not weigh.
And the seasons are more laced veils than reality bite.
If you had loved me at my best I think you
could have loved me forever
though I have learnt not to wallow in grief
over your absence.

It is through seeing in myself
everything you will have to miss
I am learning to appreciate them more.
To allow the honey of my gasp to live on my tongue
and savour the sweetness.
On a day not unlike every other this winter,
learning to live without your fireplace comfort,
I made herbal tea.
I read Virginia Woolf.
I stamped my body with a heart of approval
labelled *me*.
I will never mourn myself for not being.

Spit Kintsugi

So, there's this thing, right?
And it's something everyone has the tendency to do
but for those with a certain predisposition
it's like default factory settings —
Like you're sat on a concrete street
looking up at plant laden balconies,
dreaming of living the life
of those who lounge on metal Ikea chairs
and smoke too many cigarettes for someone of 23.
You can see the life you've always wanted, but
you haven't yet managed to configure the plans
for an elevator, or stairs, or even a fucking ladder.
Like you don't yet have the capabilities to rise up,
the right methods and mechanisms
to help yourself get to where everyone else is.
But of course, that's not the whole truth.
Because there's people on the balconies too,
with worn-out copies of *The Stranger*
who have been locked outside for hours
because they forgot the key to the French doors.
Returning to the point, when you've lost the key,
(can't quite conjure a ladder)
you can only make do with what you have.
And what you have is this black-and-white thinking:
It's either there or it's not.
You're either in love or you're not.
And that sounds like the view of a toddler
when you phrase it like that, understandably so.
Three year-olds have a better grasp of nuance than I do
when you go more than two days without replying to my text.
I'm not trying to excuse my erratic behaviour,
simply offer an explanation.

Like when documentaries devote thirty minutes
to exploring Manson's troubled childhood or
how Dahmer lacked affection and attachments.
I'm fairly sure the BBC isn't trying to excuse murder
in the same way I now see calling you
a bottom-feeding, insufferable, Bear Grylls-wannabe cunt
was maybe not the best reaction.
There's this feeling when you leave me
that I want to turn around and proclaim
that we have only known each other for 72 hours
but I would capture the whole sun within my throat
and allow it to reduce my voice to cinders
if it meant I could hear you saying the words
I love you, just once.
I'd never need to reply because when the rays began to shine
through my singed craw, the light would grace your shadow
and you'd know.
I've thought about leaping from the door
when you're driving down country roads,
just so my last memory would be your knuckles
pressed white as you switch gears
and the small white scar on your left forefinger
I never had the chance to ask you about.
Because maybe if you told me, it would ruin it forever,
if I let the mundane creep in and ruin the myth
of you that foxtrots across my prefrontal cortex.
Some days I wake up,
I go about my routine,
I eat, I drink, I bathe,
but until your name flashes across my phone
it's as if no-one had bothered
to turn any of the lights in this house on.

I live in the dim until the spark ignites and you
are light, you are sunshine, you are energy, and
healing, and love, and life and whole —
and I don't even know your middle name.
We talk and we travel and we climb rocks
on beaches by the shed you're going to buy to renovate.
You ask me whether I like my stepfather
over bad beer and single Jack and Diet Cokes.
In an ideal word I would have skirted over all
the gritty details on our first date.
I would have waited for you to ask me out again
before prying and pushing myself onto your agenda.
I would have told you *goodnight*
instead of telling you to pull off on the side of the road.
I would have held my tongue when I was nervous
about whether you liked me before the third date.
I would have fallen asleep with ease
instead of replaying your goddamn smile over and over
until it was a broken track, disjointed and ugly,
gnarling with a gaze I can no longer tell is friendly.

But I'm not a balcony person,
and the first time you spent 24 hours
without the urge to consume me,
to greedily feast upon my sardonic messages
I plummeted
further and further until you were simply a bystander
to my plunge.
When I begin to piece my shattered bones back together
a kintsugi of tobacco and Budweiser spit
any prints you had left on my shards have been
removed like a graze.

And it was probably my own fault
for nosediving into you so deeply
when we were simply testing the waters,
but it's the only way I know how to be.

If you had looked more closely
you might have seen the grouting
cementing me together
from everyone else who I would have captured the sun for,
or the moon, or the stars.

It's not that you aren't special
or that what we had wasn't real —
It was as real as the absurd.
But when you see like I do
there are blindfolds made of petals and
sunglasses of thorns
and while the blind can climb mountains
I'll never be able to ascend in the way you need.

Sillage

I dab you on like perfume,
leaving kisses strewn across every point
where the flesh is stretched tight,
revealing all the places you could hurt me
but you've spared me the final blow.
Vulnerability is the way my bed still smells like
you, even now.
Amber vials with vanilla hues
the line between sweet and sour is a disposable strip;
Lemon sherbet dotted across my neckline.

Sol

I searched the bible for your name.
All I found was stories of creation
like I hadn't already seen the birth of the world
in the crack of your crooked teeth.
Solomon spoke wisdom like the tombs
your tongue has inscribed beneath my skin
to the remains you nestled;
your impetuous grin is the skip of my heartbeat
when you draw me in.
The insipid, tumultuous race
of a neglected child,
the organ I have let revolt
and kettled in
cries out for you.

I am reborn in your image

Like White Musk and Cigarette Smoke

Like white musk and cigarette smoke.
That's how I remember my mother always smelling
and she didn't even start smoking 'til I was maybe ten,
after the boys came around to the front of my house
waiting for my brother to appear
so they could fight him
for whatever reason only fourteen year-old boys know.
For the stress, she claimed.
She did what mothers do.
She bottled her agony
and tried to find a way
to let it out with every drag
and exhale
and I never really got it
'til my denim jacket started smelling like
You want a cig?
and I was rolling up my terror
in papers and filters,
nicotine-scented fingers
trembling with every inhale.
I don't want to romanticise the tools of my demise
but I think I've started smelling like my mum.
And maybe, more than the actual act of smoking,
that's a comfort.
It helps.

I Know I Could Be Good

A man who made magic out of words once told
me that things were

built for a future which never happened.

I feel like I am *things*, which is frustrating
because I can't even come up with the words
myself, so I have to steal the reels that come
flowing eloquently out of his brain
because mine was made only to mirror,
            to mimic the rhetoric that others find so
easily, like conjuring worlds can be done with a
single breath ( )

and in the exhale I see the figments of a
fictional paradise, a place where maybe I could
not have to think but I feel like to him it's as
natural as the tide and their ease to speak and to
grab the right words is done like the water
snatching seashells from the shore and
returning them in abundance because the ocean
has never made an unfair trade/

like no one else has to worry about whether
their shallow breath is an unfair trade,

like I'm stealing gasps ( ) from people who
deserve to partake more than I do, their delight
a triumph over every evil — *who am I to deny
them that just for my pathetic fright —*

and like every tic and every shake is taking up
more space than I should be allowed and with
plants, with plants when they begin to grow in
undesirable ways and the roots threaten to
         dis   rupt the perfectly even ground
we pluck, and we trim, and we tend to put their
expansion

to an end and I wonder why no-one has yet
plucked my hands from the air as I try to
explain what seems like really a very simple
concept to me that I just can't quite muster
from my brain.

Is there something to looking in the mirror and
not seeing yourself? Every few months or so
I
    lose
         me.   I wish

I was better at remembering who it is I am
supposed to be.

I just recreate new versions, adding new
characters when the last save doesn't work
(can't we go back to the original?). There's
nothing I miss more than me.

Sometimes I wake — like everyone does — in the
middle of the night — when so many others are
awake — with the starry sky transcribed, saucers

as syllables, and planet punctuation but once
again the art of losing comes too easily to me.

I was put here with all these words and all this
beauty inside, and then things happened. And
it almost doesn't matter what it was that
happened... Because they happened. And now?
it's like my fingers aren't made to flip the

switch, to release the flood and I know, I know
they could be good.
I can feel it. But I was built for a future which
never happened. Now I'm just borrowing
words.

Ophelia Damnation

My friend and I spend our evenings
screaming at God,
throwing profanities at the sky to rain down,
finding new vices
to help bring about the inevitable,
knocking years off like
bottles from the brick wall
at the bottom of the garden
that we climb, high on wine
and that indestructible bliss.
I decipher figures of future
lovers in the grey pollution
and she laughs, not believing
in prophecy or divine intervention,
throwing bouquets of cigarette butts
behind her as we walk. Pink skies above,
swigging beatnik blood,
postponing Ophelia damnation
in her bath of red.
As I write, poised on her back doorstep,
the keyboard rattles off
blasphemous lamentations
of the non-believers, cursing the sublime
for how the ash falls,
we are children with God complexes
preaching to atheists. I tend
to her wounds speckled in their chianti tones,
filling them with Indian ink and misguided
prayers,
trying to make sure this year stays
scarlet in every letter I type.
As the pious, cruelly-cast stones

at our paper knees bloodied from the night,
I allow her confessions of every past
transgression to grace the concrete below.
They don't know you like I do;
they don't realise
just how very mortal you are.
But right now, in this moment
we are mortaled, mottled
beyond belief, stretching the nights
past the blush of the sky.
Eventually, morning will come,
announced by bitter brews and
ever-so-slightly sore heads
and we will have to face all
we have confessed.
But for now, the word *Bastard* echoes,
for now, there is no regret,
for now, there is nothing
to pay penance for,
for now, we will not
seek forgiveness
and we laugh.
My friend and I spend our evenings
screaming at God.
Throwing profanities at the sky to rain down,
finding new vices
to help bring about the inevitable.
And we laugh.

Mother, Maid and Mixed Martial Arts

Betwixt my heart
bareback warrior
sword in cat-tails
and dust in the crevices of your furrowed brow
not anger
no
not disdain
just confusion —
How do you get here?
Betwixt my heart
burrowed inside
made a fortress of fortifications
and flayed skin,
my lungs cocoon you
and you age
grow
grow old
your legs soon stretch
past the length of my own
birth from the soles of my feet
I am slain
and you are infant victor

Love

I don't know what love is.

        I'm 22 years old. I'm basically a child in the grand scheme of things. But some people don't make it to 22. Some people love more in 22 years than others do in 88.

I can count on one hand how many people have loved me	and not hurt me.

How many people have held me
without crushing me with the same arms.

I don't know what love is.

But I know it's not so different from hurt.

I know that love and hate are a funambulist's dream,

and it is not just Philippe Petit strung between the Twin Towers.

I don't know if God exists, but I know love does.

        Like I know the wind will blow and sometimes it will knock us down.

        Like I know the tide will come back and sometimes it will take us with it.

AGAPE

                        Like I know I will
                        continue to write and
                        sometimes it will be
                        good and sometimes it
                        will be bad.

I don't know what love is.

But I've been in it,
   I've felt it,   I've
      had it given to me.

I'm terrified of it but I cannot let it go.

I don't know what love is, but I think it's

absurd
     comfort in

   haphazard
      occupation.

The familiar,
     tender
        sustenance.

Finding protection
                in the
             burgeoning
     contamination.

Being   momentarily
    vulnerable in the

evertaking
    indestructible bliss.
I don't know what love is.

But I think it is this.

Acknowledgements

This book is a meditation on love and there's no way it would have come to fruition (or even be sent out to be read by Bent Key) without my love, Sol. I'm so lucky to have found you and I'm eternally grateful for all your support. I couldn't have done this without you. I love you.

I have to thank my best friend Kieran. At the start of this year, you came to see me perform for the first time. Afterward, you said you couldn't wait to be in the acknowledgments of my first book. So here it is, buddy. I love you.

I also can't send this book into the world without thanking my favourite queer rays of sunshine. Jack, Simon, Laura, Jay: thank you for everything. I love my little family.

Finally, the master of words and prose poetry, my former Master's tutor Oz Hardwick: I'll be forever grateful for your advice and support.

About the Author

Caitlin Mckenna is a queer, socialist, vegan poet from Leeds, West Yorkshire. After writing throughout her entire life she decided to pursue poetry while at University. Since 2020 she's been published in a number of anthologies and journals, nominated for a Pushcart Prize, and included on a CLMP reading list.

A spoken-word artist as well as a poet, she's often found performing around the area and attending as many literary events as possible. Caitlin is a lover primarily — especially of cats, slasher films, and the beautiful people she's met along the way.

About Bent Key

It started with a key.

Bent Key is named after the bent front-door key that Rebecca Kenny found in her pocket after arriving home from hospital following her car crash. It is a symbol of change, new starts, risk and taking a chance on the unknown.

Bent Key is a micropublisher with ethics. We do not charge for submissions, we do not charge to publish and we make space for writers who may struggle to access traditional publishing houses, specifically writers who are neuro-divergent or otherwise marginalised. We never ask anyone to write for free, and we like to champion authentic voices.

All of our beautiful covers are designed by our graphic designer Sam at SMASH Design & Illustration, a graphic design company based in Southport, Merseyside.

Find us online:
bentkeypublishing.co.uk

Instagram & Facebook   @bentkeypublishing
Twitter   @bentkeypublish